Simple Blessings in
PATCHWORK

13 Traditional Projects with a Twist

by **Jill Shaulis** and **Vicki Olsen**
of Yellow Creek Quilt Designs

SIMPLE BLESSINGS IN PATCHWORK: 13 TRADITIONAL PROJECTS WITH A TWIST

Text copyright © 2016 by Jill Shaulis and Vicki Olsen

Photography and artwork copyright © 2016 by C&T Publishing, Inc.

Publisher: Amy Marson
Creative Director: Gailen Runge
Editor: Kimber Mitchell
Technical Editor: Jane Miller
Book Designer: Bob Deck
Illustrator: Eric Sears
Photographer: Aaron Leimkuehler

Published by Kansas City Star Quilts, an imprint of C&T Publishing, Inc.,
P.O. Box 1456, Lafayette, CA 94549

KANSAS CITY STAR QUILTS
an imprint of C&T Publishing

Library of Congress Cataloging-in-Publication Data
Shaulis, Jill and Olsen, Vicki

Library of Congress Control Number: 2016933692

Simple Blessings in Patchwork: 13 Traditional Projects with a Twist

ISBN 978-1-61745-454-7 (soft cover)
eBook ISBN 978-1-61745-442-4

Printed in the United States of America by Walsworth Publishing Co., Marceline, MO

Table of Contents

About the Authors 3

Introduction 4

Dedication 4

Acknowledgments 5

Tools of the Trade 6

About the Projects 6

PROJECTS

Simple Blessings 7

Time Savvy 24

Starstruck 29

A Star is Born 33

Chocolate-Covered Blueberries 37

Scrap Happy 41

Fanfare 46

Fresh Picked 56

Petals in the Wind 66

Stepping Back in Time 71

ABOUT THE AUTHORS

Jill Shaulis (left) and Vicki Olsen (right) learned to sew from their mom and participated in 4-H and Home Economics. Jill made her first quilt as a history project when she was in junior high. The two began quilting in earnest in the late 1980s and opened their shop, Sew Many Antiques, in their hometown of Pearl City, Illinois, in 1992. They now design patterns for their quilt shop, Yellow Creek Quilt Designs, which was featured in *Quilt Sampler* magazine in 2011. Jill expanded her creative talents in 2015 by designing fabrics for Windham Fabrics. Her first two fabric lines, Kindred Spirits I and Kindred Spirits II, are just the beginning of more civil war reproductions to come. As a bonus to those fabric lines, Jill and Vicki created a club called Kindred Spirits. Many shops across the country and beyond have participated in it with great success. Jill and her husband Dave make their home in Lanark, Illinois, and have six children. Vicki and her husband Dave make their home in Pearl City, Illinois, and have three children.

Introduction

Inspired by our Grandma Stroup and our mom's never idle hands, we have both sewn since we were little and often made our own clothes. Although she did not quilt, our grandma was a wonderful seamstress and an accomplished needleworker. Our mom is also a talented seamstress and made most of our clothing when we were kids. The quilting bug hit us after Jill invited our mom to attend a beginning quilt class with her in 1989. Once Vicki saw what we were doing, she quickly jumped in. We haven't stopped quilting since!

As quilt designers, tradition has always guided our creative process. Whether we're browsing an antique quilt booth at a quilt show or exploring photos of old quilts online, we find ourselves drawn to these treasures of the past. Perhaps it's their warm colors or their connection to the busy hands of yesterday's quilters who were able to do so much with so little. Thankfully, many of these quilted treasures have endured the test of time and are still cherished today.

Despite our love of tradition, we can't resist putting our own twist on it. For example, traditional sampler quilts often feature only pieced blocks, but we like to give them a fresh look by combining pieced blocks with wool appliqué as illustrated in our *Simple Blessings* quilt. We also enjoy adapting block designs into smaller projects such as table runners like *Fresh Picked*, abloom with wool posies in pieced basket blocks. English paper-pieced hexagons take an inventive twist in two delightful small table toppers that meld cotton prints with the warmth of wool. Searching for a project to give your piecing skills a workout? A series of pieced row designs create a striking pattern of cotton petals and classic Churn Dashes in *Petals in the Wind*. Need to whittle down that overflowing scrap bag? Put it to good use with *Scrap Happy*, a black-and-red beauty that showcases Four-Patch units made with an astounding variety of prints. All of these refreshing twists on tradition and many more await you in this book. We hope you'll find the perfect project among them—or better yet, so many that you won't know where to start!

Happy Quilting,

Jill   Vicki

Dedication

This book is dedicated to our dear friend, Pauline Miller, who always referred to us as the sisters she never had. We felt so blessed when she paid us this compliment and are honored to call her "sister". We think of her every time we see a fabric that's "just plain pretty", a "make-you-happy" batik, or a wool-stitched sheep. And our hearts smile whenever we hear one of her favorite artists, Kid Rock, sing. Cancer took her in a few short weeks but even more time could not have prepared us for her loss. Along with her many friends and family, we miss her bubbly personality and warm smile every day. Here's to you, Pauline!

Acknowledgments

Our heartfelt thanks go to:
Todd Hensley for giving us this opportunity to write a book with such a wonderful company.

Kimber Mitchell for making the book production process such a pleasure. We can't imagine a better editor. You made this entire process such a pleasure!

Aaron Leimkuehler for your amazing photographic skills and insight.

Our designer Bob Deck for bringing our projects to life on the pages of this beautiful book.

Our illustrator Eric Sears for your artistic talents creating all the helpful diagrams that make our projects easier to follow.

Our technical editor Jane Miller for your keen eye in verifying the accuracy of our instructions.

Windham Fabrics and Marcus Brother Textiles for fulfilling our fabric requests.

Dan Kolbe and Margaret Knoup for beautifully quilting several projects in this book—sometimes on very short notice!

Our dedicated quilt shop employees who are always there even at a moment's notice to help out in any way.

Our friends, customers, fellow quilt shop owners and designers who have supported and encouraged our quilting habits.

Jill Shaulis
To my heart and soul, my husband Dave. With warmth and understanding, he has supported me through euphoric highs and stressful moments. Through it all, he has never complained about fixing meals or keeping up with the laundry and household chores. He always supports me, takes pride in my passion and has come to understand that my brain doesn't necessarily turn off even when the lights do!

I don't know how someone truly thanks a mom as wonderful as mine. I'm so blessed to have her constant support and love. Knowing how proud she is of me means the world to me.

I can't begin to express my thanks to my children Todd, Scott, and Jodi. They have helped out in our quilt shop since they were small. Today, Todd and Scott tirelessly lend their guidance, creativity and computer skills. Jodi, who is already an accomplished quilter and excellent sales person, is always there when I need a sounding board or any other assistance.

And to Vicki who shares my passion for sewing, which has been such a huge part of our lives. Thanks for being a part of this book.

Vicki Olsen
I must thank my husband for enduring so many hours alone while I "play" in my sewing room. He continues to take care of the cooking and other chores while I create and in the process, he makes sure I don't go hungry or thirsty. He is always a reliable sounding board even when he's not completely sure what I'm talking about!

To my daughter Sara who has always appreciated what I do and is just starting to get bitten by the quilting bug.

To my daughter-in-law Dawn who is a wonderful quilter and has honored me by making several of my designs.

To my mom and sister who got me started quilting in the first place. Thanks, Jill, for continuing to challenge me and keep me motivated. For that, I am grateful!

TOOLS OF THE TRADE

As quilters, we all have tools we like to use that make the quilting process go smoother. Here are some of the handy helpers we used to make some of the featured quilts in this book.

To quickly and easily square up Hourglass units like the ones featured in *Simple Blessings* on Page 7, *A Star Is Born* on Page 33 and *Time Savvy* on Page 24, we like to use the handy **Precision Trimmer 6**.

We often use spray sizing on our blocks because it gives them a crisp look and feel, making them easier to work with. Our favorite is **Mary Ellen's Best Press**.

For projects like our *Chocolate-Covered Blueberries* and *Starstruck* on Pages 29 and 37, we love using pre-cut hexagon papers by **Paper Pieces** because they are extremely accurate and can be reused several times.

When foundation-piecing detailed patterns like *Stepping Back in Time* on Page 71, we prefer to use a base product called **Fundation**, which holds up much better than paper when piecing such small projects.

For projects like *Fanfare* on Page 46, the **Easy Dresden** ruler offers a great alternative to the provided templates.

ABOUT THE PROJECTS

Half-Square Triangle Units
Throughout the book, the instructions allow for the half-square triangle units to be made larger then trimmed down for accuracy but feel free to make them with your preferred method.

Borders
Border measurements listed in the cutting instructions for each project are guidelines. Because of variances in individual sewing techniques, it is best to assemble your quilt center and measure it before cutting your borders the exact size needed for your quilt.

Binding
We cut our binding three inches wide and sew it to the quilt with a ⅜" seam allowance to make turning corners easier. As a result, our binding turns out perfectly every time. Feel free to use whatever binding width you prefer.

SIMPLE BLESSINGS

Designed and pieced by Jill Shaulis
Quilted by Dan Kolbe

Finished quilt size: 39" x 39"

Finished block size: 9" x 9"

This sampler quilt not only combines my favorite quilting elements, such as wool appliqué and classic pieced blocks, but also serves as a reminder of what I hold most dear in life—family, faith, hope and love.

Fabric Requirements

◈ 2 yards tan print for blocks, first border and Flying Geese border
◈ 8–10 fat quarters in assorted green, blue, blue/black, red, gold, brown, black and plum prints for blocks
◈ 6½" x 12" dark green wool for "Faith" "Hope" "Love" and "Family"
◈ 4" x 9" brown wool for cross
◈ 2" x 4" gold wool for fish
◈ 5" x 9" brown wool for tree
◈ 4" x 6" green wool for leaves
◈ 4" x 6" cream wool for doves
◈ 3" square red wool 1 for top heart
◈ 2" x 2½" red wool 2 for middle heart
◈ 3½" square red wool 3 for bottom heart
◈ 1 yard green print for Flying Geese border, outer border and binding
◈ Fusible web

Cutting Instructions

Templates have been reversed. For block number references, see the quilt assembly diagram on Page 20. Because felted wool does not fray, there is no need to turn under the edges of the appliqué pieces.

1. Trace the templates on Pages 21-23 the number of times noted on Pages 10 and 11 onto the paper side of fusible web, leaving approximately ¼" between tracings.

2. Cut out each shape just outside the drawn lines.

3. Following the fusible web manufacturer's instructions, press the fusible web templates onto the wrong side of the appropriate-color wools.

4. Cut out each shape on the drawn lines, then remove the fusible web backing.

BLOCK 1:
From tan print, cut:
◈ 2 — 4½" squares
◈ 8 — 2" squares

From red print, cut:
◈ 2 — 4½" squares

From gold print, cut:
◈ 1 — 3½" square

From black print, cut:
◈ 4 — 3½" squares

BLOCK 2:
From tan print, cut:
◈ 3 — 2½" squares
◈ 4 — 1½" x 2½" rectangles
◈ 4 — 1½" squares
◈ 1 — 3½" x 6½" rectangle
◈ 1 — 3½" x 9½" rectangle

From green print, cut:
- ◈ 4 — 1½" x 2½" rectangles

From red print, cut:
- ◈ 4 — 2½" squares

From blue/black print, cut:
- ◈ 4 — 1½" squares
- ◈ 2 — 2½" squares

From dark green wool, cut:
- ◈ 1 of "Faith" template

From gold wool, cut:
- ◈ 1 of Template A for fish

From brown wool, cut:
- ◈ 1 of Template B for cross

BLOCK 3:

From tan print, cut:
- ◈ 4 — 3½" squares
- ◈ 1 — 2" x 17" strip

From blue print, cut:
- ◈ 1 — 3½" square (this should be a darker blue)
- ◈ 1 — 2" x 17" strip (this should be a darker blue)

From brown print, cut:
- ◈ 8 — 2" squares

BLOCK 4:

From tan print, cut:
- ◈ 4 — 2½" squares
- ◈ 8 — 1½" squares
- ◈ 1 — 3½" x 6½" rectangle
- ◈ 1 — 3½" x 9½" rectangle

From green print, cut:
- ◈ 1 — 1½" x 2½" rectangle
- ◈ 1 — 1½" x 3½" rectangle

From blue print, cut:
- ◈ 1 — 1½" x 2½" rectangle
- ◈ 1 — 1½" x 3½" rectangle

From red print, cut:
- ◈ 1 — 1½" x 2½" rectangle
- ◈ 1 — 1½" x 3½" rectangle

From brown print, cut:
- ◈ 1 — 1½" x 2½" rectangle
- ◈ 1 — 1½" x 3½" rectangle

From green wool, cut:
- ◈ 39 of Template C for leaves

From brown wool, cut:
- ◈ 1 of Template D for tree

From dark green wool, cut:
- ◈ 1 of "Family" template

BLOCK 5:

From tan print, cut:
- ◈ 2 — 4½" squares
- ◈ 8 — 2" x 3½" rectangles

From green print, cut:
- ◈ 2 — 4½" squares

From blue print, cut:
- ◈ 8 — 2" squares

From red print, cut:
- ◈ 1 — 3½" square
- ◈ 8 — 2" squares

BLOCK 6:

From tan print, cut:
- ◈ 12 — 1½" squares
- ◈ 4 — 1½" x 2½" rectangles
- ◈ 2 — 2½" squares
- ◈ 1 — 3½" x 6½" rectangle
- ◈ 1 — 3½" x 9½" rectangle

From blue print, cut:
- ◈ 3 — 2½" squares
- ◈ 4 — 1½" x 2½" rectangles

From red print, cut:
- ◈ 8 — 1½" squares
- ◈ 6 — 2½" squares

From gold print, cut:
- ◈ 2 — 2½" squares

From dark green wool, cut:
- ◈ 1 of "Hope" template

From cream wool, cut:
- ◈ 1 of Template E for dove
- ◈ 1 of Template F for dove

BLOCK 7:
From tan print, cut:
- ◈ 4 — 2" squares
- ◈ 4 — 3" squares
- ◈ 2 — 5" squares

From blue print, cut:
- ◈ 1 — 3½" square
- ◈ 4 — 3" squares

From red print, cut:
- ◈ 2 — 5" squares

From gold print, cut:
- ◈ 4 — 2" squares

BLOCK 8:
From tan print, cut:
- ◈ 1 — 2½" square
- ◈ 8 — 1" squares
- ◈ 12 — 1½" squares
- ◈ 1 — 3½" x 6½" rectangle
- ◈ 1 — 3½" x 9½" rectangle

From green print, cut:
- ◈ 4 — 1½" x 2½" rectangles
- ◈ 8 — 1½" squares

From blue/black print, cut:
- ◈ 4 — 1½" x 2½" rectangles

From red print, cut:
- ◈ 12 — 1½" squares

From dark green wool, cut:
- ◈ 1 of "Love" template

From red wool 1, cut:
- ◈ 1 of Template G for top heart

From red wool 2, cut:
- ◈ 1 of Template H for middle heart

From red wool 3, cut:
- ◈ 1 of Template I for bottom heart

BLOCK 9:
From tan print, cut:
- ◈ 4 — 2" squares
- ◈ 4 — 2" x 3½" rectangles
- ◈ 4 — 2½" squares

From assorted green prints, cut:
- ◈ 4 — 2" squares
- ◈ 1 — 3½" square

From plum print, cut:
- ◈ 4 — 2" x 3½" rectangles

From black print, cut:
- ◈ 4 — 2½" squares

BORDERS:
From tan print, cut:
- ◈ 36 — 2¼" x 4" rectangles for Flying Geese border
- ◈ 4 strips the width of fabric for first border (cutting size will be determined in the sewing instructions)

From green print, cut:
- ◈ 74 — 2¼" squares for Flying Geese border
- ◈ 4 — 2½" strips the width of fabric for outer border
- ◈ 4 — 3" strips the width of fabric for binding

Sewing Instructions

BLOCK 1

1. Draw a diagonal line from corner to corner on the wrong side of the 2 — 4½" tan print squares.

2. With right sides together, layer a marked 4½" tan print square on top of a 4½" red print square, sew ¼" from both sides of the drawn line, then cut on the drawn line to yield two half-square triangle units. Press seams toward the red print, then trim the units to measure 3½" square. Repeat to create a total of four half-square triangle units.

3. Draw a diagonal line from corner to corner on the wrong side of the 8 — 2" tan print squares.

4. With right sides together, layer a 2" tan print square on top of a 3½" black print square. Sew on the drawn lines, trim ¼" from the sewing line of the tan print square only as shown in the second diagram below, then press the resulting triangle back. Repeat on the adjacent corner as shown below. (**Note:** The triangles will overlap to create a seam allowance.) Repeat to make a total of four units.

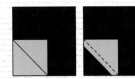

5. Sew together four units from step 4, four units from step 2 and 1 — 3½" gold print square to complete the block.

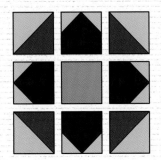 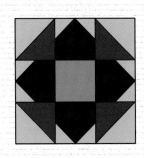

BLOCK 2

1. Sew together 1 — 1½" x 2½" tan print rectangle and 1 — 1½" x 2½" green print rectangle. Press seam toward the green print. Repeat to make a total of four units.

2. Draw a diagonal line from corner to corner on the wrong side of the 2 — 2½" tan print squares.

3. Referring to step 2 of the Block 1 section, use the 2 — 2½" tan print squares and 2 — 2½" blue/black print squares to create a total of four half-square triangle units. Press seams toward the blue/black print.

4. Cut each half-square triangle unit from step 3 diagonally from corner to corner as shown below.

5. Cut each of the 4 — 2½" red print squares diagonally from corner to corner.

6. With right sides together, center a unit from step 4 on top of a unit from step 5. (**Note:** The red triangle may be slightly larger.) Sew a ¼" seam allowance along the diagonal side, press seam toward the red print, then trim the unit to measure 1½" square. Repeat to create a total of four units.

7. Sew together two units from step 6, 1 — 1½" blue/black print square and 1 — 1½" tan print square to create the following unit. Repeat to create a total of four units.

8. Sew together four units from step 1, four units from step 7 and 1 — 2½" tan print square to create the following unit.

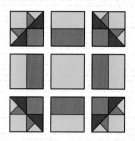 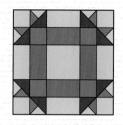

9. Referring to the following diagram, sew the 3½" x 6½" tan print rectangle to the right side of the unit from step 8, then sew the 3½" x 9½" tan print rectangle to the bottom of that unit.

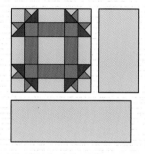 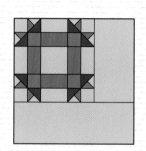

10. Referring to the project photo on Page 8 for placement, use a blanket stitch and thread that matches the appliqué to appliqué the wool cross, fish and "Faith" to the quilt block.

Blanket Stitch

BLOCK 3

1. With right sides together, sew the 2" x 17" tan strip to the 2" x 17" dark blue print strip. Press seam toward the dark blue print. Trim one end straight, then sub-cut the strip set into 8 — 2" x 3½" segments. (**Note:** to keep your strip set square, align a ruler line with the seam line after a couple cuts and make sure the straight end is still straight. If not, trim before continuing.)

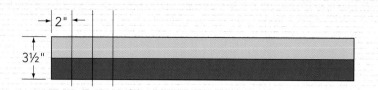

2. Sew together two of the segments from step 1 to create a Four-Patch unit. Repeat to make a total of four units.

3. Using the method noted in step 4 of the Block 1 section, use 8 — 2" brown print squares and 4 — 3½" tan print squares to create a total of four of the following units.

4. Sew together four units from step 2, four units from step 3 and 1 — 3½" dark blue print square to complete the block.

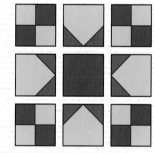 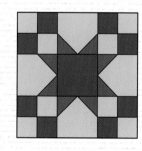

BLOCK 4

1. Draw a diagonal line on the wrong side of the 8 — 1½" tan print squares.

2. With right sides together, layer a marked 1½" tan print square on one end of 1 — 1½" x 2½" green print rectangle. Sew on the drawn line, trim the tan print square only ¼" away from the sewing line, then press the resulting triangle back. (**Note:** If your tan print is too light, you may have to forgo trimming so the dark fabric doesn't show through.) Repeat with the 1½" x 2½" red, blue and brown print rectangles to create a total of four units.

3. Repeat step 2 with 1 — 1½" tan print square and 1 — 1½" x 3½" red print rectangle, noting the different orientation of the drawn diagonal lines on the tan print squares below. Repeat with the 1½" x 3½" green, blue and brown print rectangles to create a total of four units.

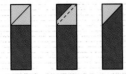

4. Sew together a unit from step 2, a unit from step 3 and 1 — 2½" tan print square to create the following unit. Referring to the diagram in step 5 for color cues, repeat to make the remaining three units using the brown/red, blue/green and brown/blue combinations.

5. Sew together the four units from step 4 to create the following unit.

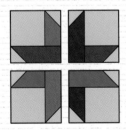 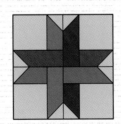

6. Sew the 3½" x 6½" tan print rectangle to the right of the unit from step 5, then sew the 3½" x 9½" tan print rectangle to the bottom of that unit.

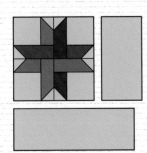 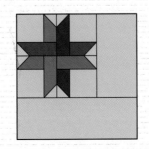

7. Referring to the project photo on Page 8 for placement, use a blanket stitch and thread that matches the appliqué to appliqué the tree and "Family" to the quilt block. (Because the leaves are so small, you can simply sew a straight stitch down their centers.)

BLOCK 5

1. Draw a diagonal line from corner to corner on the wrong side of the 2 — 4½" tan print squares.

2. Referring to step 2 of the Block 1 section, use the two marked tan print squares and 2 — 4½" green print squares to make a total of four half-square triangle units. Press seams toward the green print, then trim the units to measure 3½" square.

3. Draw a diagonal line on the wrong side of the 8 — 2" red print squares and 8 — 2" green print squares.

4. With right sides together, layer a marked 2" red print square on top of 1 — 2" x 3½" tan print rectangle. Sew on the drawn line, trim ¼" from the sewing line of the red square only, then press the resulting triangle back. Repeat on the other side to create a Flying Geese unit. Repeat to create a total of four red/tan Flying Geese units.

5. Repeat step 4 with the 8 — 2" blue print squares and 4 — 1" x 3½" tan print rectangles to create a total of four blue/tan Flying Geese units.

6. Sew a unit from step 4 to the top of a unit from step 5. Repeat to create a total of four units.

7. Sew together four units from step 2, four units

from step 6 and 1 — 3½" red print square to complete the block.

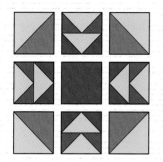 

BLOCK 6

1. Using the method noted in step 4 of the Block 5 section, use 4 — 1½" x 2½" tan print rectangles and 8 — 1½" red print squares to create a total of four Flying Geese units.

2. Using the method noted in step 4 of the Block 5 section, use 4 — 1½" x 2½" blue print rectangles and 8 — 1½" tan print squares to create a total of four Flying Geese units.

3. Sew a unit from step 2 to the top of a unit from step 1. Repeat to create a total of four units.

4. Referring to the method noted in step 2 of the Block 1 section, use 2 — 2½" blue print squares and 2 — 2½" red print squares to make a total of four half-square triangle units. Trim the units to measure 1½" square.

5. Draw a diagonal line from corner to corner on the wrong side of the 2 — 2½" tan print squares and 2 — 2½" gold print squares.

6. Referring to the method noted in step 2 of the Block 1 section, use 2 — 2½" tan print squares

and 2 — 2½" red print squares to create a total of four half-square triangle units.

7. Referring to the method noted in step 2 of the Block 1 section, use 2 — 2½" gold print squares and 2 — 2½" red print squares to create a total of four half-square triangle units.

8. Cut each of the units from steps 6 and 7 diagonally from corner to corner.

9. Sew together one red/gold print triangle and one tan/red print triangle from step 8 to create the following unit. Repeat to create a total of eight units. Trim these units to measure 1½" square.

10. Sew together one unit from step 4, two units from step 9 and 1 — 1½" tan print square to create the following unit. Repeat to create a total of four units.

11. Sew together the four units from step 3, the four units from step 10 and 1 — 2½" blue print square to create the following unit.

12. Sew the 3½" x 6½" tan print rectangle to

the right of the unit from step 11, then sew the 3½" x 9½" tan print rectangle to the bottom of that unit.

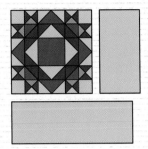 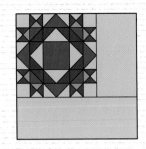

13. Referring to the project photo on Page 8, use a blanket stitch and thread that matches the appliqué to appliqué the doves and "Hope" to the block.

BLOCK 7

1. Referring to the method noted in step 2 of the Block 1 section, use 4 — 3" tan print squares and 4 — 3" blue print squares to create a total of eight half-square triangle units. Trim the units to measure 2" square.

2. Sew together two units from step 1, 1 — 2" tan print square and 1 — 2" gold print square to create the following unit. Repeat to create a total of four units.

3. Referring to the method noted in step 2 of the Block 1 section, use 2 — 5" tan print squares and 2 — 5" red print squares to make a total of four half-square triangle units.

4. Cut the units from step 3 in half diagonally as shown in the below left diagram, then sew two halves together as shown in the below right

diagram. Trim the units to measure 3½" square. Repeat to create a total of four units.

5. Sew together the four units from step 2, the four units from step 4 and 1 — 3½" blue print square to complete the block.

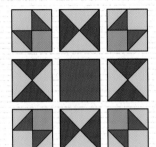 

BLOCK 8

1. Draw a diagonal line on the wrong side of the 8 — 1" tan print squares.

2. With right sides together, layer a marked 1" tan print square in the top corner of a 1½" red print square. Sew on the drawn line, trim ¼" from the sewing line of the tan print square only, then press the resulting triangle back. (**Note:** If your tan print is too light, you may have to forgo trimming so the dark fabric does not show through.) Repeat to make a total of eight units.

3. Sew together two units from step 2, 1 — 1½" tan print square and 1 — 1½" red print square to create the following unit. Repeat to make a total of four units.

4. Referring to the method noted in step 4 of the Block 5 section, use 4 — 1½" x 2½" green print rectangles and 8 — 1½" tan print rectangles to make a total of four Flying Geese units.

5. Referring to the method noted in step 4 of the Block 5 section, use 4 — 1½" x 2½" blue/black print rectangles and 8 — 1½" green print squares to make a total of four Flying Geese units.

6. Sew a unit from step 4 to the top of a unit from step 5. Repeat to make a total of four units.

7. Sew together the four units from step 3, the four units from step 6 and 1 — 2½" tan print square to create the following unit.

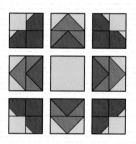 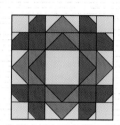

8. Sew the 3½" x 6½" tan print rectangle to the right side of the unit from step 7, then sew the 3½" x 9½" tan print rectangle to the bottom of that unit.

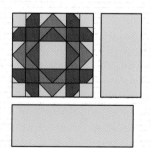 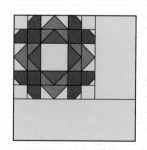

9. Referring to the project photo on Page 8, use a blanket stitch and thread that matches the appliqué to appliqué the three hearts and "Love" to the quilt block.

BLOCK 9

1. Draw a diagonal line from corner to corner on the wrong side of the 4 — 2½" tan print squares.

2. Referring to the method noted in step 2 of the Block 1 section, use the marked 4 — 2½" tan print squares and the 4 — 2½" black print squares to make a total of eight half-square triangle units. Trim the units to measure 2" square.

3. Sew together two units from step 2, 1 — 2" tan print square and 1 — 2" green print square to make the following unit. Repeat to make a total of four units.

4. Sew 1 — 2" x 3½" plum print rectangle to 1 — 2" x 3½" tan print rectangle. Repeat to make a total of four units.

5. Sew together four units from step 3, four units from step 4 and 1 — 3½" green print square to complete the block.

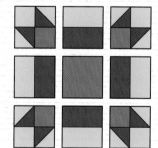 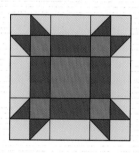

QUILT CENTER

Referring to the quilt assembly diagram on Page 20, sew the nine blocks into rows, then join the rows to complete the quilt center.

FLYING GEESE BORDER

1. Referring to the method noted in step 4 of the Block 5 section, use the 36 — 2¼" x 4" tan print rectangles and 72 — 2¼" green print squares to make a total of 36 Flying Geese units.

2. Sew together nine Flying Geese units to make a row. Repeat to make a second row.

3. Sew together nine Flying Geese units to make a row, then sew 1 — 2¼" green print square to each end of the row. Repeat to make a second row.

FIRST BORDER

1. To determine the width of the side border strips, measure the two border strips from step 3 of the Flying Geese Border section from end to end, then subtract 4" to eliminate the corner squares. Measure the quilt center from side to side through the center. Subtract the quilt center measurement from the border measurement, then divide that number by two and add ½". Cut two tan print border strips this size by the width of fabric.

2. To determine the width of the top and bottom border strips, measure the two border strips from step 2 of the Flying Geese Border section from end to end, then measure the quilt top from top to bottom through the center. Subtract the quilt top measurement from the border measurement, then divide that number by two and add ½". Cut two tan print border strips this size by the width of fabric.

3. Measure the quilt top from top to bottom through the center, then trim two side border strips from step 1 to match that measurement. Referring to the quilt assembly diagram, sew those two strips to the sides of the quilt top.

4. Measure the quilt top from side to side through the center, then trim the two border strips from step 2 to match that measurement. Referring to the quilt assembly diagram, sew those two strips to the top and bottom of the quilt center.

COMPLETING THE QUILT

1. Sew the two border strips from step 2 of the Flying Geese Border section to the sides of the quilt top.

2. Sew the two border strips from step 3 of the Flying Geese Border section to the top and bottom of the quilt top.

3. Measure the quilt top from top to bottom through the center, then cut two 2¼" green print strips to match that measurement. Referring to the quilt assembly diagram, sew those two strips to the sides of the quilt top.

4. Measure the quilt top from side to side through the center, then cut two 2¼" green print strips to match that measurement. Referring to the quilt assembly diagram, sew those two strips to the top and bottom of the quilt top.

5. Sandwich the quilt top, batting and backing; baste. Quilt as desired, then bind.

Quilt Assembly Diagram

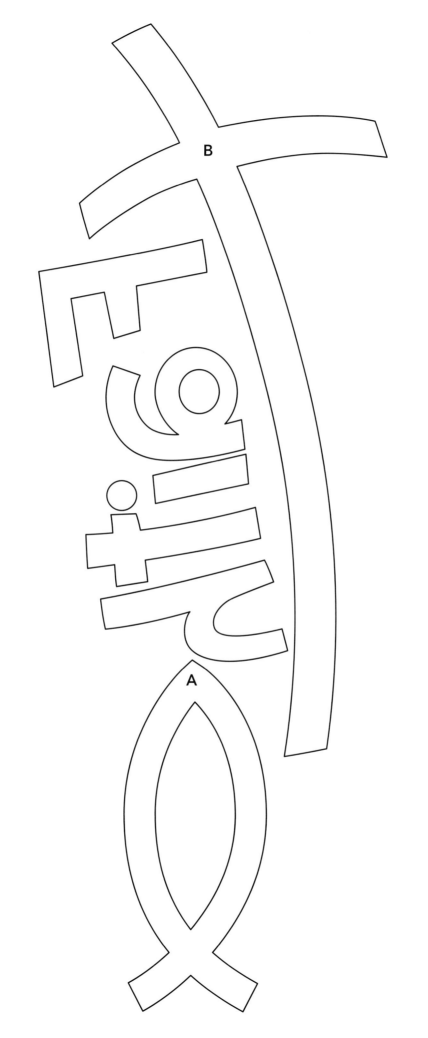

B

A

TIME SAVVY

Designed and pieced by Vicki Olsen
Quilted by Margaret Knoup

Finished quilt size: 54" x 72"

Finished block size: 8" x 8"

I love trying new methods of making quilt blocks, and I found a great time-saving technique for making the Hourglass blocks in this quilt. There are 140 Hourglass units in this design, and you will be amazed by how quickly they come together.

Fabric Requirements

◈ ¼ yard each of nine light prints for blocks
◈ ¼ yard each of nine medium to dark prints for blocks
◈ 1 yard black marble for sashing
◈ ¼ yard black print for sashing cornerstones
◈ 1 yard black floral for border
◈ 3½ yards fabric of choice for backing
◈ ⅔ yard black floral for binding

Cutting Instructions

From each light print, cut:
◈ 2 — 8" squares (Keep like squares together.)

From each medium to dark print, cut:
◈ 2 — 8" squares (Keep like squares together.)

From black marble, cut:
◈ 4 — 8½" strips the width of fabric, then sub-cut those into 82 — 1½" x 8½" strips for sashing

From black print, cut:
◈ 2 — 1½" strips the width of fabric, then sub-cut those into 48 — 1½" squares for sashing cornerstones

From black floral, cut:
◈ 7 — 4½" strips the width of fabric for border
◈ 7 — 3" strips the width of fabric for binding

Sewing Instructions

BLOCKS

1. Select a light print and medium to dark print to pair together. With right sides together, layer the 8" light print and 8" medium to dark print square. Sew a ¼" seam around the perimeter of the layered pair. Press to set the seams. Repeat with a second matching pair that uses the same fabrics as the first set sewn.

2. Make four cuts on the units from step 1 to yield a total of eight units from each pair. Press each unit to the dark print.

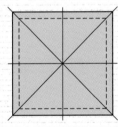 

3. Sew together two units from step 2, then trim the resulting unit to measure 4¼" square. (I like to use the Precision Trimmer 6 for squaring them.) Repeat with the remaining units from step 2.

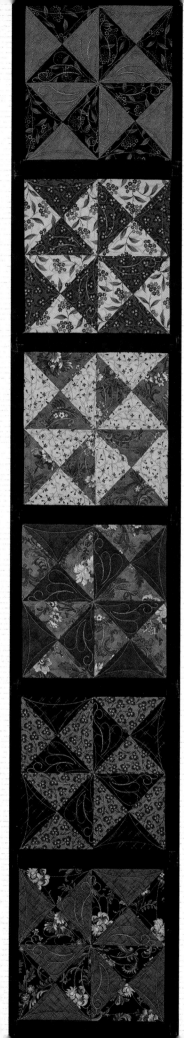

4. Sew the matching sets of units from step 3 to create two Hourglass blocks, which should measure 8½" square each.

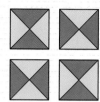

5. Repeat steps 1–4 to create a total of 35 blocks. (You will have one extra block, which can be incorporated into a quilt label, if you wish.)

QUILT ASSEMBLY

1. Referring to the quilt assembly diagram on Page 28, lay out the Hourglass blocks, black marble sashing strips and black print sashing cornerstones in 15 rows.

2. Sew together a row of 5 — 8½" Hourglass blocks alternating with 6 —1½" x 8½" black marble sashing strips. Press seams toward the sashing strips. Repeat to create a total of seven rows.

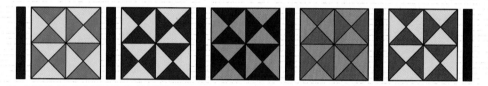

3. Sew together a row of 5 — 1½" x 8½" black marble sashing strips alternating with 6 — 1½" black print square sashing cornerstones. Press seams toward the sashing strips. Repeat to create a total of eight rows.

4. Join the rows from steps 2 and 3 to complete the quilt center.

5. Make 2 — 4½" x 64½" black floral border strips. Referring to the quilt assembly diagram, sew these two strips to the sides of the quilt center. Press seams toward the border.

6. Make 2 — 4½" x 54½" black floral border strips. Referring to the quilt assembly diagram, sew these two strips to the top and bottom of the quilt top. Press seams toward the border.

7. Sandwich the quilt top, batting and backing; baste. Quilt as desired, then bind.

Quilt Assembly Diagram

STARSTRUCK

Designed and made by Jill Shaulis

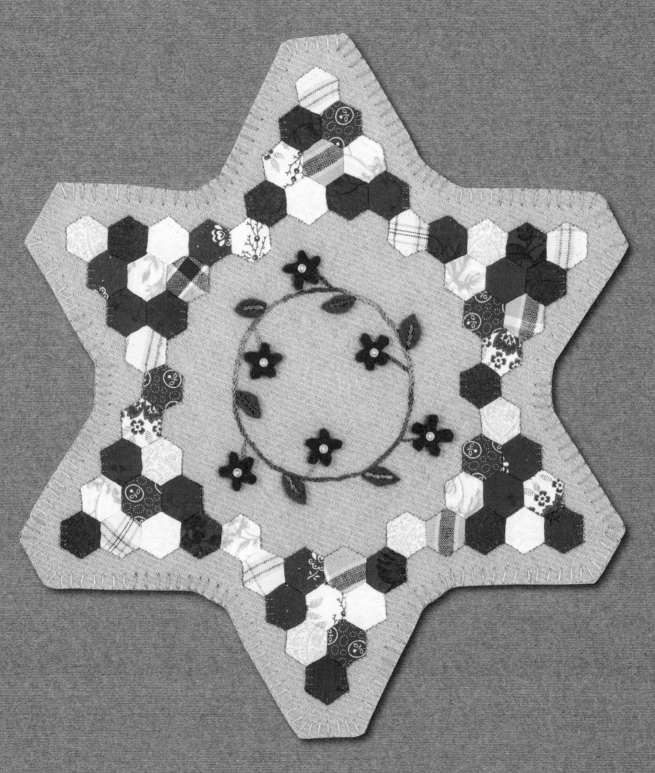

Finished size: 11½" x 11½"

Adorned in a star-studded mix of hexagons and a flowery show of wool appliqué, this dazzling design will be the talk of the tabletop.

Fabric Requirements

- 1 — 1⅜" x 10" each of five red prints for hexagons
- 1 — 1⅜" x 10" each of six medium/light cream prints for hexagons
- 12½" square tan wool for appliqué background
- 2" x 3" red wool for flowers
- 1" x 3" green wool for leaves
- 12½" square fabric of choice for backing
- Size 12 perle cotton to match green and tan wool
- ⅜ yard fusible web
- Six micro cream buttons

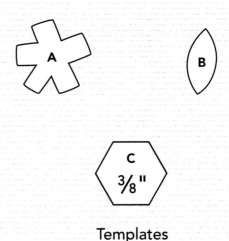

Templates

Cutting Instructions

Because felted wool does not fray, there is no need to turn under the edges of the appliqué pieces.

1. Trace the templates above the number of times noted below onto the dull side of freezer paper, leaving approximately ¼" between tracings.

2. Cut out each shape just outside the drawn lines.

3. Using the wool setting of your iron, press the shiny side of the freezer-paper templates onto the right side of the appropriate-color wools.

4. Cut out each shape on the drawn lines, then remove the freezer paper.

From each red print, cut:
- 6 — 1⅜" squares for hexagons

From each medium/light cream print, cut:
- 6 — 1⅜" squares for hexagons

From red wool, cut:
- 6 of Template A for flowers

From green wool, cut:
- 6 of Template B for leaves

Sewing Instructions

1. Clip the corners of the 1⅜" squares, being careful not to trim the entire piece to ¼" from the edge of the hexagons because it is best to have a little extra fabric to work with. It is OK if the fabric overlaps a bit on the back of the hexagons. Don't worry about cutting the squares a precise size because the clipping is designed only to reduce the bulk that goes to the back of the hexagons.

2. Thread your needle with a single contrasting thread and make a knot at the end. (I prefer to use one needle to baste and a different one to whipstitch because the template will dull the basting needle.) Lay the hexagon template above on the wrong side of the fabric and fold over the seam allowance on one side. Insert the needle through the fabric and template from the right side of the fabric. Fold the seam allowance over to the next side, then insert the needle down from the wrong side to the right side. Fold the seam allowance over to the next side. Continue in the same manner until all sides are basted. End with a thread tail on the right side of the hexagon, which will make the paper hexagon easier to remove later.

3. Following the method noted in step 2, continue basting all 66 hexagons. Use 60 of them to create six of the units shown below. (The remaining six hexagons will be used later to join these units.)

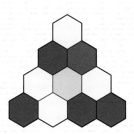

4. To join the hexagons, place them side by side. (Do not place them right sides together when stitching them because the stitching will be visible when you open them flat.) Using a contrasting thread to make your stitches easier to see, make a knot at the end. Starting at a point on the wrong side, slide your needle between the fabric and template to hide the knot in the fold through the fabric from both hexagons, being careful to catch only the fabric and not the template. Lay the two pieces flat, make a loop knot to connect both hexagons, and whipstitch along the sides you are joining. Make a loop knot at the next point. Continue adding hexagons around the first/middle hexagon until you've created a unit like the one shown in step 3. Repeat to create a total of six of those units.

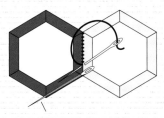

You can also slide the needle under/inside the fold to start the next piece.

5. Referring to the following diagram, join the sections stitched in step 4 with the remaining six hexagons. Do not remove the template pieces yet because they provide stability while stitching.

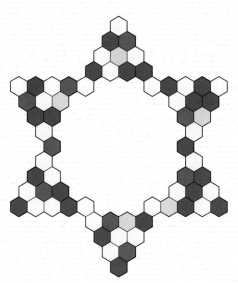

6. Lay the unit from step 5 on the fusible web and carefully trace around it. Cut out the fusible web just inside the drawn line. Using fabric sizing spray, press the unit.

7. Carefully remove the basting and the templates. Press again. Apply the fusible web to the wrong side of the hexagon design. (It does not need to extend completely to the edge of the hexagons.) Center and fuse the hexagon design to the 12½" tan wool square.

8. Using clear invisible thread on the top of your sewing machine and a lighter thread in the bobbin, machine-sew a blanket stitch around the entire outer and inner perimeter of the hexagon design to attach it to the tan wool square. (Alternatively, you can hand-sew a blanket stitch with silk thread.)

9. Draw a 3" diameter circle in the center of the unit from step 8. Using a stem stitch and green perle cotton, stitch the circle and the flower stems.

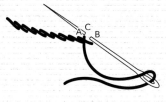

Stem Stitch

10. Referring to the project photo on Page 29 for placement, stitch the flowers in place with a micro button in their centers. Stitch the leaves in place with a stem stitch through their centers.

11. Referring to the fusible web manufacturer's instructions, apply fusible web to the wrong side of the backing fabric. Center the backing over the project top and fuse.

12. Trim all sides of the tan wool square ½" from the outer points of the hexagons, being particularly careful when cutting the inside corners. (You want a line at the base of those corners, not a point.) Cut the outer points off last.

13. Using a blanket stitch and tan perle cotton, sew around the perimeter of the tan wool star.

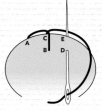

Blanket Stitch

A STAR IS BORN

Designed and pieced by Jill Shaulis
Quilted by Dan Kolbe

Finished quilt size: 59½" x 78½"

Finished block size: 8½" x 8½"

I love star blocks, especially those that are traditional with a little twist. I put my own inventive spin on the blocks in this quilt by making the Hourglass units rectangular instead of the usual square. When combined with the block's Snowball center, the overall effect looks more complex than it actually is!

Fabric Requirements

- ◈ 1¾ yards cream print for block backgrounds
- ◈ 1⅞ yards blue print for blocks
- ◈ 1 yard caramel print for blocks
- ◈ ¾ yard brown print for sashing
- ◈ ⅛ yard caramel print for sashing cornerstones
- ◈ 1⅜ yard blue print for border
- ◈ 4¾ yards fabric of choice for backing
- ◈ ¾ yard blue print for binding

Cutting Instructions

From cream print, cut:
- ◈ 140 — 3" squares for blocks
- ◈ 35 — 5" squares for blocks

From blue print, cut:
- ◈ 35 — 4" squares for blocks
- ◈ 70 — 5" squares for blocks
- ◈ 7 — 6" strips the width of fabric for border
- ◈ 7 — 3" strips the width of fabric for binding

From caramel print, cut:
- ◈ 35 — 5" squares for blocks
- ◈ 140 — 1½" squares for blocks
- ◈ 48 — 1½" squares for sashing cornerstones

From brown print, cut:
- ◈ 82 — 1½" x 9" strips for sashing

Sewing Instructions

BLOCKS

1. Draw a diagonal line on the wrong side of each 5" cream print square and each 5" caramel print square.

2. With right sides together, layer a 5" cream print square on top of a 5" blue print square. Sew ¼" from both sides of the drawn line. Cut on the drawn line to create two half-square triangle units. Press toward the blue print. Repeat to create a total of 70 half-square triangle units.

3. Repeat step 2 for the 5" caramel print squares and 5" blue print squares to make a total of 70 half-square triangle units.

4. With right sides together, layer one half-square triangle unit from step 2 on top of one half-square triangle unit from step 3, cut diagonally from corner to corner, then stitch a ¼" seam along each cut line as shown in the diagram below right. Repeat to make a total of 140 of these units.

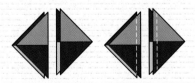

5. Press open the seam of the unit from step 4, then trim the resulting Hourglass unit to measure

4" square. Repeat to make a total of 140 of these units.

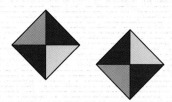

6. Trim the side of a unit from step 5 with the caramel fabric to 3" tall. (**Note:** It is important to square the unit to 4" square *before* trimming it in this step or the intersection of the four points might not be correct.) Repeat to make a total of 140 of these units, which should measure 3" x 4".

7. Draw a diagonal line on the wrong side of 140 — 1½" caramel squares.

8. With right sides together, layer 4 — 1½" caramel squares on the four corners of a 4" blue print square. Sew a thread away from the outer side of the drawn line in each of the four caramel squares, trim ¼" away from the stitching in the four caramel squares, then press the resulting triangles back. (**Note:** I do not trim the blue square because if my stitching isn't exact, I can use it as a guide when stitching the other sections to this unit later.) Repeat to make a total of 35 of these units.

9. Referring to the following diagram, sew together one unit from step 8, four units from step 6 and 4 — 3" cream print squares to create a block. Press the first seams toward the center and cream print squares. Press the last two seams away from the center or open. Repeat to make a total of 35 blocks.

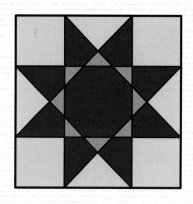

QUILT ASSEMBLY

1. Referring to the quilt assembly diagram on Page 36, lay out the star blocks, brown print sashing strips and caramel print sashing cornerstone squares in 15 rows.

2. Sew together a row of five star blocks alternating with 6 — 1½" x 9" brown print sashing strips. Press seams toward the sashing strips. Repeat to create a total of seven rows.

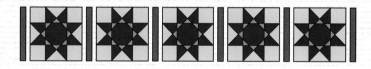

3. Sew together a row of 5 — 1½" x 9" brown print sashing strips alternating with 6 — 1½" caramel print square sashing cornerstones. Press seams toward the sashing strips. Repeat to create a total of eight of these rows.

4. Join the rows from steps 1 and 2 to complete the quilt center.

5. Make 2 — 6" x 68" blue print border strips. Referring to the quilt assembly diagram, sew these two strips to the sides of the quilt center. Press seams toward the border.

6. Make 2 — 6" x 60" blue print border strips. Referring to the quilt assembly diagram, sew these two strips to the top and bottom of the quilt top. Press seams toward the border.

7. Sandwich the quilt top, batting and backing; baste. Quilt as desired, then bind.

Quilt Assembly Diagram

CHOCOLATE-COVERED BLUEBERRIES

Designed and made by Jill Shaulis

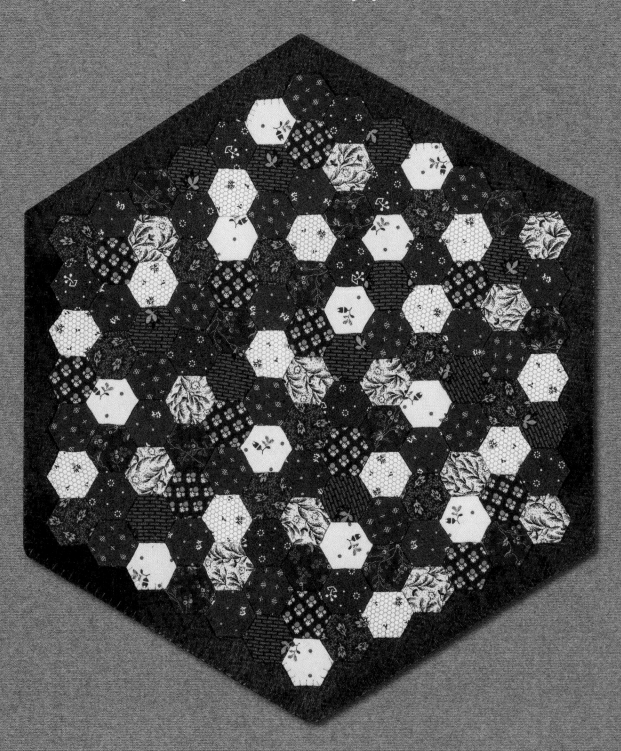

Finished size: 11¼ " x 13"

Treat yourself to this delightful table topper, which mingles the warmth of wool with a harmonious medley of cotton hexagons.

Fabric Requirements

◈ 1¾" x WOF (width of fabric) each of three blue prints for hexagons
◈ 1¾" x WOF each of three cream prints for hexagons
◈ 1¾" x WOF each of four brown prints for hexagons
◈ 15" square brown wool for appliqué background
◈ 15" square fabric of choice for backing
◈ 13" square fusible web
◈ Size 12 perle cotton in color that matches brown wool

Cutting Instructions

From each blue print, cut:
◈ 14 — 1¾" squares for hexagons

From each cream print, cut:
◈ 14 — 1¾" squares for hexagons

From one brown print, cut:
◈ 10 — 1¾" squares for hexagons

From three brown prints, cut:
◈ 11 — 1¾" squares for hexagons

½"

Template

Sewing Instructions

1. Clip the corners of the 1¾" squares, being careful not to trim the entire piece to ¼" from the edge of the hexagons because it is best to have a little extra fabric to work with. It is OK if the fabric overlaps a bit on the back of the hexagons. Don't worry about cutting the squares a precise size because the clipping is designed only to reduce the bulk that goes to the back of the hexagons.

2. Thread your needle with a single contrasting thread and make a knot at the end. (I prefer to use one needle to baste and a different one to whipstitch because the template will dull the basting needle.) Lay the hexagon template below left on the wrong side of the fabric and fold over the seam allowance on one side. Insert the needle through the fabric and template from the right side of the fabric. Fold the seam allowance over to the next side, then insert the needle down from the wrong side to the right side. Fold the seam allowance over to the next side. Continue in the same manner until all sides are basted. End with a thread tail on the right side of the hexagon, which will make the paper hexagon easier to remove later.

3. Following the method noted in step 2, continue basting all 127 hexagons.

4. To join the hexagons, place them side by side. (Do not place them right sides together when stitching them because the stitching will be visible when you open them flat.) Using a contrasting thread to make your stitches easier to see, make a knot at the end. Starting at a point on the wrong side, slide your needle between the fabric and template to hide the knot in the fold through the fabric from both hexagons, being careful to catch only the fabric and not the template. Lay the two pieces flat, make a loop knot to connect both hexagons, and whipstitch

along the sides you are joining. Make a loop knot at the next point. Continue adding hexagons around the first/middle hexagon until you've used all 127 basted hexagons.

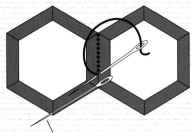

You can also slide the needle under/inside the fold to start the next piece.

5. Once a hexagon is surrounded on all sides by other hexagons, remove the basting from the one that is surrounded, then remove the template but do NOT remove the basting/template from any outer edges.

6. Trace the outline of the hexagon design from step 5 onto the fusible web.

7. Using fabric sizing spray, press one side of the hexagon design. Carefully remove the basting and the templates on that side only. Press again. Continue with the remaining five sides, one side at a time.

8. Apply the fusible web to the wrong side of the hexagon design.

9. Center the hexagon design on the center of the 15" square brown wool piece, then fuse it in place.

10. Using smoke-colored invisible thread in the top of your sewing machine and a dark thread in the bobbin, machine-sew a blanket stitch around the entire perimeter of the hexagon design to attach it to the brown wool square. (Alternatively, you can hand-sew a blanket stitch with silk thread.)

11. Referring to the fusible web manufacturer's instructions, apply fusible web to the wrong side of the backing fabric. Center and fuse the wrong side of the backing fabric to the wrong side of the unit from step 10.

12. Using a ruler as a straight edge, trim each side of the brown wool square ½" from the outer point of the hexagons.

13. Using brown perle cotton, hand-sew a blanket stitch around the outer perimeter of the brown wool hexagon.

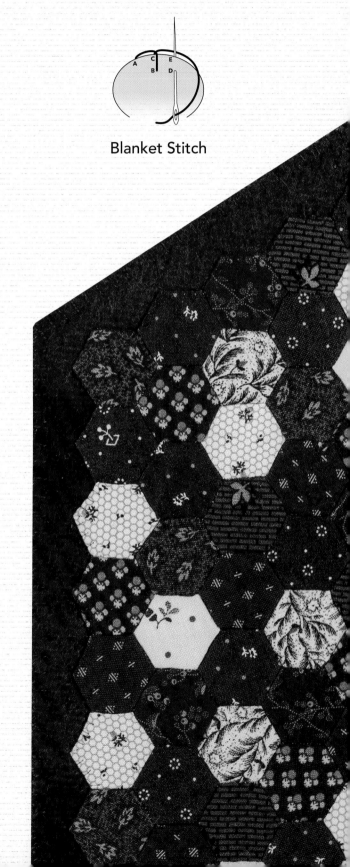

Blanket Stitch

SCRAP HAPPY

Designed and pieced by Vicki Olsen
Quilted by Margaret Knoup

Finished quilt size: 62½" x 74½"

Finished block size: 6" x 6"

I love the simplicity of traditional quilt patterns and the way scraps of fabric transform them into a one-of-a-kind beauty. The combination of black and red has always been a favorite of mine. For this design made of Four-Patch units, I opted for a multitude of reproduction prints to create a truly scrappy look.

Fabric Requirements

I used fat quarters for the red, black and light prints—44 reds, 44 blacks and 63 lights—for the blocks.

◈ 1⅜ yards total of assorted red prints for blocks and second border
◈ 1⅜ yards total of assorted black prints for blocks and second border
◈ 1⅓ yards total of assorted tan, cream and white prints for blocks
◈ 1¼ yards tan print for first, second and third borders
◈ 1⅛ yards black print for outer border
◈ ¾ yard black print for binding
◈ 4 yards fabric of choice for backing

TIP:
To dress up your quilt backing, make extra Four-Patch units to combine with other fabric. Don't forget to include a label with special details about your quilt (including the quiltmaker) so future generations will know its history.

Cutting Instructions

From assorted red prints, cut:
◈ 50 — 1½" x 22" strips for blocks and second border

From assorted black strips, cut:
◈ 50 — 1½" x 22" strips for blocks and second border

From assorted tan, cream, and white prints, cut:
◈ 36 — 2½" x 22" strips, then sub-cut those into 284 — 2½" squares for blocks

From tan print, cut:
◈ 16 — 2½" strips the width of fabric, then cut 50 — 2½" squares and set aside remaining strips and partial strip for first and third border

From black print, cut:
◈ 8 — 4½" strips the width of fabric for outer border
◈ 8 — 3" strips the width of fabric for binding

Sewing Instructions

BLOCKS
1. Using one 1½" x 22" red and one 1½" x 22" black strip, sew 50 strip sets. Sub-cut each strip set into 14 — 1½" x 2½" segments.

2. Sew the units from step 1 into 338 Four-Patch units. (You will need 284 of them for the blocks

— 32 sets of five of them and 31 sets of four of them. The remaining 54 will be used in the border.)

3. Using the 284 Four-Patch units from step 2 and the 284 — 2½" tan, cream and white print squares, make 32 of Block A and 31 of Block B.

   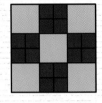

Block A   Block B

QUILT CENTER

1. Referring to the quilt assembly diagram on Page 45, lay out the 32 Block As and 31 Block Bs in nine rows of seven blocks each. Begin with a Block A in the odd numbered rows and a Block B in the even numbered rows.

2. Sew the blocks from step 1 into rows, then join the rows to complete the quilt center, which should measure 42½" x 54½".

FIRST BORDER

1. Sew together three of the 2½" tan print strips end to end. Repeat with another three tan print strips. From each strip, cut 1 — 2½" x 54½" strip and 1 — 2½" x 46½" strip.

2. Referring to the quilt assembly diagram, sew the 2 — 2½" x 54½" tan print strips to the sides of the quilt center. Then sew the 2 — 2½" x 46½" tan print strips to the top and bottom of the quilt top.

SECOND BORDER

1. Alternating 15 Four-Patch units and 14 — 2½" tan print squares, make two side border strips.

2. Alternating 12 Four-Patch units and 11 — 2½" tan print squares, make two strips. Then sew a Four-Patch unit to each end of those two strips to make the top and bottom border strips.

3. Referring to the quilt assembly diagram, sew the two strips from step 1 to the sides of the quilt top. Then sew the two strips from step 2 to the top and bottom of the quilt top.

THIRD BORDER

1. Sew together three of the 2½" x WOF tan print strips end to end. Repeat with another three tan print strips. From each strip, cut 1 — 2½" x 62½" strip and 1 — 2½" x 54½" strip.

2. Referring to the quilt assembly diagram, sew the 2 — 2½" x 62½" tan print strips to the sides of the quilt top. Then sew the 2 — 2½" x 54½" tan print strips to the top and bottom of the quilt top.

OUTER BORDER

1. Sew together the 8 — 4½" x WOF black print strips end to end, then cut that strip to make 2 — 4½" x 62½" strips and 2 — 4½" x 66½" strips.

2. Referring to the quilt assembly diagram, sew the 2 — 4½" x 66½" black print strips to the sides of the quilt top. Then sew the 2 — 4½" x 62½" black print strips to the top and bottom of the quilt top.

Sandwich the quilt top, batting and backing; baste. Quilt as desired, then bind.

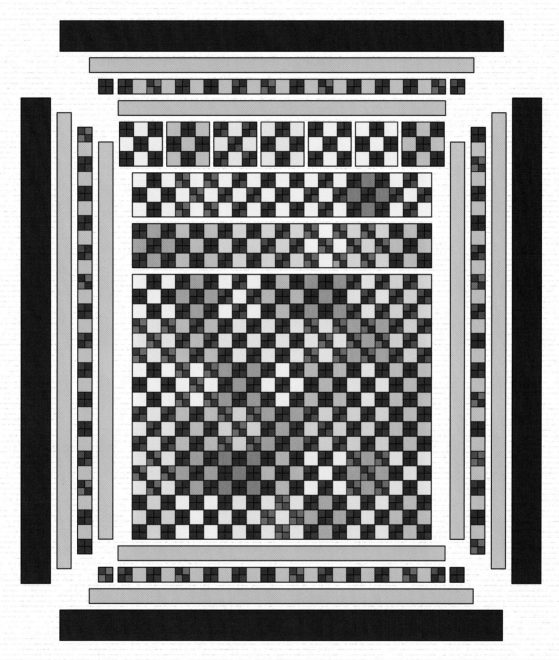

Quilt Assembly Diagram

FANFARE

Designed and pieced by Jill Shaulis
Quilted by Dan Kolbe

Finished large quilt size: 39" x 49"

Finished small quilt size: 28" x 28"

Finished large block size: 7" x 7"

Finished small block size: 4½" x 4½"

Several years ago, I mocked up this design but struggled to create clean points on the fan blades with needleturn appliqué. The technique featured in this quilt makes quick work of that step with simple machine stitching.

Fabric Requirements

I made a large version (pictured on Page 53) and a small version (pictured on Page 47) of this quilt. Unless otherwise noted, yardage amounts for the small version are listed in parentheses below. For the large version, I used the same rose print for the setting triangles, outer border and binding.

◈ 1 yard cream print for block backgrounds (⅓ yard)
◈ 1½ yards total of dark prints for fan blades (17—5" squares)
◈ ¼ yard brown print for fan bases (⅛ yard)
◈ ⅝ yard rose print for setting triangles (¼ yard)
◈ ¼ yard green print for inner border in large version only
◈ ⅝ yard rose print for outer border in large version only
◈ ⅝ yard brown print for first and outer borders in small version only
◈ ⅛ yard teal print for second border in small version only
◈ 2½ yards fabric of choice for backing (⅞ yard)
◈ ½ yard rose print for binding (⅓ yard brown print)
◈ ¼ yard fusible interfacing (⅛ yard)

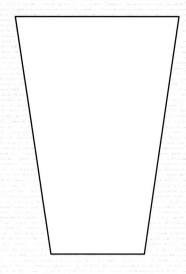

Small Version Template

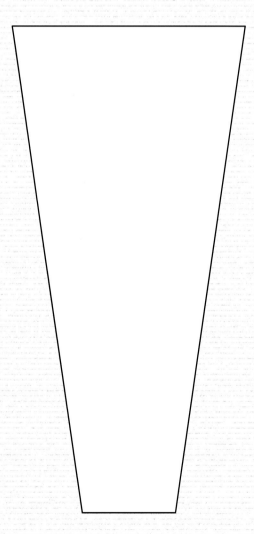

Large Version Template

Cutting Instructions

Unless otherwise noted, cutting instructions for the small version are listed in parentheses below. Setting triangles are oversized and will be trimmed to size later.

From cream print, cut:
- 18 — 7½" squares for block backgrounds (13 — 5" squares)

From dark prints, cut:
- 90 — 3" x 6" rectangles, then cut one wedge template on Page 48 from each rectangle for fan blades (From each of the 17 — 5" squares, cut four wedge templates on Page 48 to yield a total of 65 fan blades.)

From brown print and interfacing, cut:
- 5 — 6"-diameter brown circles for fan bases (4 — 4"-diameter brown circles)

From rose print, cut:
- 3 — 11½" squares, then cut each square diagonally twice from corner to corner to yield a total of 12 setting triangles (2 — 8" squares to yield a total of eight setting triangles)
- 2 — 6¼" squares, then cut each square diagonally once from corner to corner to yield a total of four corner triangles (2 — 4½" squares to yield a total of four corner triangles)
- 2 — 4" x 42½" strips for outer border in large version only
- 2 — 4" x 39½" strips for outer border in large version only
- 5 — 3" strips the width of fabric for binding in large version only

From green print, cut:
- 2 — 1½" x 40½" strips for inner border in large version only
- 2 — 1½" x 32½" strips for inner border in large version only

From brown print, cut:
- 2 — 1½" x 20" strips for first border in small version only

- 2 — 1½" x 22" strips for first border in small version only
- 2 — 3¼" x 23" strips for outer border in small version only
- 2 — 3¼" x 28½" strips for outer border in small version only
- 3 — 3" strips the width of fabric for binding in small version only

From teal print, cut:
- 2 — 1" x 22" strips for second border in small version only
- 2 — 1" x 23" strips for second border in small version only

Sewing Instructions

Unless otherwise noted, measurements for the small version are listed in parentheses in the following instructions.

BLOCKS

1. With right sides together, fold the dark print wedges in half lengthwise, stitch a ¼" seam across the top and backstitch at the end with the fold, clip that corner, and finger-press the seam open. Turn the wedge right side out, using a point turner to gently push out the point. From the wrong side, ensure the seam is centered and that it stays open. Press in place.

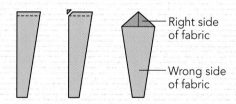

Right side of fabric

Wrong side of fabric

2. Sew together five fan blades, then press the seams open. Repeat to create a total of 18 fans for the large version or 13 fans for the small version.

3. Position each fan on a 7½" cream print square (5" cream print square) so that the two raw edges of the fan blades are flush with the edges of the background square, then pin it place. Using smoke-colored monofilament thread in the top of your sewing machine and dark thread in the bobbin, machine-appliqué the fans in place with a blanket stitch. (If you prefer, you can hand-appliqué them.)

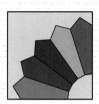

4. With right sides together, layer an interfacing circle with the bumpy (fusible) side facing the right side of the brown circle so when it's turned right side out, it can be pressed into place. Sew a ¼" seam around the outside of the layered circle and interfacing. (The fabric glides easier on the sewing machine than the interfacing, so it's best to sew with the interfacing side up.) Clip around the outer edge, fold the circle in fourths and finger-press. Cut on the fold lines to create a total of four segments. Carefully turn each quarter circle right side out, using a point turner to smooth out the curved edges. Repeat to create a total of 20 segments for the large version or 16 segments for the small version. (You will only need 18 for the large version or 13 for the small version.)

5. Place a brown segment from step 4 on one of the units from step 3 so that the curve of the brown segment covers the raw edges of the fan and the outer raw edges of the brown segment and background square align. Press until the interfacing holds it in place. (I inserted a couple pins to hold everything in place.) Then appliqué the brown segment to the fan block in the same manner used to

appliqué the fan blades. Repeat for all 18 blocks in the large version or all 13 blocks in the small version.

6. To prevent the fans from shifting when sewing the blocks together later, sew a scant ¼" seam around the outer edge of all blocks.

LARGE VERSION QUILT ASSEMBLY
1. Referring to the quilt assembly diagram on Page 54, lay out the 18 fan blocks, 10 setting triangles and four corner triangles. Sew everything except the corner triangles into rows, then join the rows. Press seams toward the setting triangles. Then sew the four corner triangles in place to complete the quilt center.

2. Because the setting triangles were oversized, trim the setting and corner triangles to ⅜" from the edges of the blocks so that the blocks appear to float within the inner border.

3. Referring to the quilt assembly diagram, sew the 2 — 1½" x 40½" green print inner border strips to the sides of the quilt center. Press seams toward the inner border. Then sew the 2 — 1½" x 30½" green print inner border strips to the top and bottom of the quilt top. Press seams toward the border.

4. Referring to the quilt assembly diagram, sew the 2 — 4" x 42½" rose print outer border strips to the sides of the quilt center. Press seams toward the outer border. Then sew the 2 — 4" x 39½" rose print outer border strips to the top and bottom of the quilt top. Press seams toward the outer border.

5. Sandwich the quilt top, batting and backing; baste. Quilt as desired, then bind.

SMALL VERSION QUILT ASSEMBLY

1. Referring to the quilt assembly diagram on Page 55, lay out the 13 fan blocks, eight setting triangles and four corner triangles. Sew everything except the corner triangles into rows, then join the rows. Press seams toward the setting triangles. Then sew the four corner triangles in place to complete the quilt center.

2. Because the setting triangles were oversized, trim the setting and corner triangles to ⅜" from the edges of the blocks so that the blocks appear to float within the inner border.

3. Referring to the quilt assembly diagram, sew the 2 — 1½" x 20" brown first border strips to the sides of the quilt center. Press seams toward the first border. Then sew the 2 — 1½" x 22" brown first border strips to the top and bottom of the quilt top. Press seams toward the first border.

4. Referring to the quilt assembly diagram, sew the 2 — 1" x 22" teal print second border strips to the sides of the quilt center. Press seams toward the second border. Then sew the 2 — 1" x 23" teal print second border strips to the top and bottom of the quilt top. Press seams toward the second border.

5. Referring to the quilt assembly diagram, sew the 2 — 3¼" x 23" brown print outer border strips to the sides of the quilt center. Press seams toward the outer border. Then sew the 2 — 3¼" x 28½" brown print outer border strips to the top and bottom of the quilt top. Press seams toward the outer border.

6. Sandwich the quilt top, batting and backing; baste. Quilt as desired, then bind.

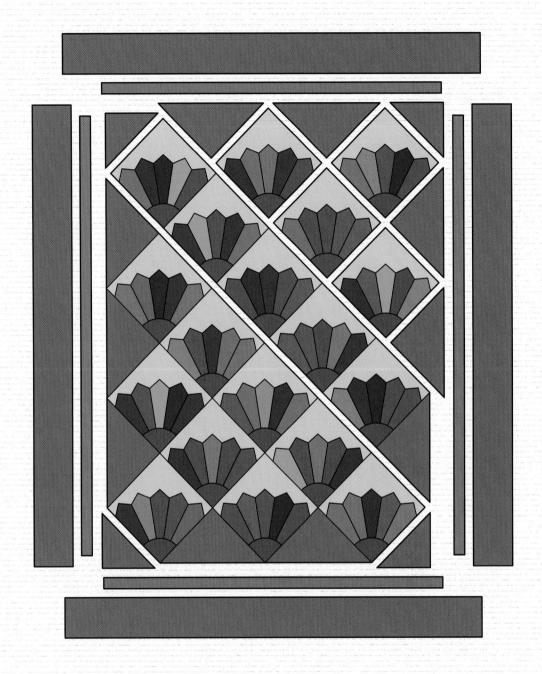

Quilt Assembly Diagram

Large Version

Quilt Assembly Diagram
Small Version

FRESH PICKED

Designed and pieced by Jill Shaulis
Quilted by Dan Kolbe

Finished table runner size:
17" x 38"

Finished wall hanging size:
12½" x 27½"

Finished table runner block size:
7½" x 7½"

Finished wall hanging block size:
5" x 5"

Abloom with freshly picked posies, this design combines my love of traditional piecing and wool appliqué. To illustrate its versatility, I made both a table runner and a wall hanging.

Fabric Requirements

I made a table runner (pictured on Page 57) and a wall hanging (pictured on Page 63). Yardage amounts for the wall hanging are in parentheses below. If only one amount is listed, the yardage applies to both versions. Inner border yardage applies only to the wall hanging.

◆ ⅓ yard light print for background
◆ ⅓ yard black print for baskets
◆ ½ yard red print for setting and corner triangles (⅜ yard)
◆ 2½" x 8" red wool for flowers (2" x 6")
◆ 2½" x 8" blue wool for flowers (2" x 6")
◆ 4" x 8" gold wool for sunflowers and red and blue flower centers (1½" x 3")
◆ 2" x 6" brown wool for sunflower centers (1½" x 4½")
◆ 3" x 6" green wool for leaves (2" x 4")
◆ ¼ yard tan print for wall hanging inner border
◆ ¼ yard green print for wall hanging inner border
◆ ⅜ yard brown/black print for outer border (¼ yard)
◆ ⅝ yard fabric of choice for backing (¼ yard)
◆ ⅝ yard brown/black print for binding (⅝ yard)
◆ Size 12 perle cotton in colors that match appliqué
◆ ⅓ yard fusible web such as Steam-a-Seam Lite (¼ yard)

Cutting Instructions

Because felted wool does not fray, there is no need to turn under the edges of the appliqué pieces. The cutting instructions for the wall hanging are listed in parentheses below. If only one amount is listed, the yardage applies to both versions.

1. Trace the templates on Page 64 the number of times noted below onto the paper side of fusible web, leaving approximately ¼" between tracings.

2. Cut out each shape just outside the drawn lines.

3. Following the fusible web manufacturer's instructions, press the fusible web templates onto the wrong side of the appropriate-color wools.

4. Cut out each shape on the drawn lines, then remove the fusible web backing.

From light print, cut:
◆ 6 — 2" x 5" rectangles for background (6 — 1½" x 3½" rectangles)
◆ 3 — 2" squares for background (3 — 1½" squares)
◆ 2 — 6" squares for background (2 — 4½" squares)
◆ 14 — 3" squares for background (14 — 2½" squares)

From black print, cut:
◆ 2 — 6" squares for baskets (2 — 4½" squares)
◆ 14 — 3" squares for baskets (14 — 2½" squares)

From red print, cut:
◆ 1 — 12¾" square (1 — 9" square), then cut it diagonally twice from corner to corner to create a total of four setting triangles
◆ 2 — 7" squares (2 — 5" squares), then cut each square diagonally once from corner to corner to create a total of four corner triangles

From tan print, cut:
- ◆ 29 — 2½" squares for wall hanging inner border
- ◆ 4 — 1½" squares for wall hanging inner border

From green print, cut:
- ◆ 29 — 2½" squares for wall hanging inner border

From brown/black print, cut:
- ◆ 2 — 3½" x 38½" strips for outer border (2 — 2¼" x 24½" strips)
- ◆ 2 — 3½" x 11½" strips for outer border (2 — 2¼" x 13" strips)
- ◆ 3 — 3" strips the width of fabric for binding

From red wool, cut:
- ◆ 3 of Template A for flowers (3 of Template H)

From blue wool, cut:
- ◆ 3 of Template B for flowers (3 of Template I)

From gold wool, cut:
- ◆ 3 of Template C for flowers (3 of Template J)
- ◆ 3 of Template D for blue flower centers (3 of Template K)
- ◆ 3 of Template E for red flower centers (3 of Template L)

From brown wool, cut:
- ◆ 3 of Template F for sunflower centers (3 of Template M)

From green wool, cut:
- ◆ 15 of Template G for leaves (15 of Template N)

Sewing Instructions

Measurements for the wall hanging are listed in parentheses below.

BLOCKS

1. Draw a diagonal line on the wrong side of the 2 — 6" light print squares (2 — 4½" squares).

2. With right sides together, layer a marked light print square from step 1 on top of a 6" black print square (4½" square). Sew a ¼" from both sides of the drawn line, cut on the drawn line, then press seams toward the black print to create two half-square triangle units. Trim the units to measure 5" square unfinished (3½" square unfinished). Repeat to create a total of four half-square triangle units. (You will only use three.)

  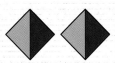

3. Draw a diagonal line on the wrong side of the 14 — 3" light print squares (14 — 2½" squares).

4. With right sides together, layer a marked light print square from step 3 on top of a 3" black print square (2½" square). Sew a ¼" from both sides of the drawn line, cut on the drawn line, then press seams toward the black print to create two half-square triangle units. Trim the units to measure 2" square unfinished (1½" square unfinished). Repeat to create a total of 27 half-square triangle units.

5. Sew a 2" half-square triangle unit (1½" square half-square triangle unit) to the end of a 2" x 5" light print rectangle (1½" x 3½" light print rectangle). Press seam toward the rectangle. Repeat to make a total of three of these two units.

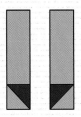

6. Sew together three 2" half-square triangle

units (1½" half-square triangle units) from step 4. Repeat to create a total of three of these units.

7. Sew together four 2" half-square triangle units (1½" half-square triangle units) from step 4. Repeat to create a total of three of these units.

8. Sew together two units from step 5, one unit from step 6, one unit from step 7, a 5" square half-square triangle unit (3½" square half-square triangle unit) and a 2" light print square (1½" square) to complete the block. Repeat to create a total of three blocks.

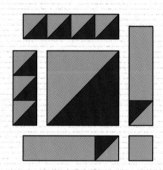

9. Using a scant ¼" seam, sew around each of the three blocks to prevent the seams from popping while appliquéing the blocks. (The scant seam will ensure the stitching does not show once the blocks are stitched together.) Referring to the project photos on Pages 57 and 63, position the wool pieces on the blocks. Using size 12 perle cotton in colors that match the appliqué, blanket-stitch the wool pieces in place. (I arranged the flowers differently in each block.) Using a darker thread, sew a French knot in the centers of the red flowers.

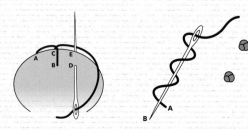

Blanket Stitch   French Knot

TABLE RUNNER ASSEMBLY

1. Lay out the three 8" square blocks, four red print setting triangles and four red print corner triangles.

2. Sew together the units from step 1, adding the four corner triangles last. When stitching the setting triangles to the blocks, begin at the square corner of the setting triangle, aligning it with the edge of the block. (The setting triangle will extend beyond the block's outer edge.) Press seams toward the setting triangles. Trim the table runner top, leaving a ⅜" seam allowance beyond the tips of the blocks. (I prefer to use a seam allowance larger than the usual ¼" so that the blocks float slightly within the border.)

3. Measure the table runner through the center from top to bottom, then cut two brown/black print border strips to match that measurement. (They should measure 3½" x 11½".) Referring to the quilt assembly diagram on Page 61, sew those two strips to the sides of the table runner.

4. Measure the table runner top through the center from side to side, including the border strips just added, then cut two brown/black print border strips to match that measurement. (They should measure 3½" x 35½".) Referring to the quilt assembly diagram, sew those two strips to the top and bottom of the table runner.

5. Sandwich the table runner top, batting and backing; baste. Quilt as desired, then bind.

Assembly Diagram

Table Runner

Assembly Diagram

Wall Hanging

WALL HANGING ASSEMBLY

1. Lay out the 3 — 5½" blocks, four red print setting triangles and four red print corner triangles.

2. Sew together the units from step 1, adding the four corner triangles last. When sewing the setting triangles to the blocks, begin at the square corner of the setting triangle, aligning it with the edge of the block. (The setting triangle will extend beyond the block's outer edge.) Do not trim the quilt top yet.

3. Referring to the half-square triangle method noted in steps 1 and 2 of the Blocks section on Page 59, make 58 — 1½" square unfinished half-square triangle units with the 29 — 2½" tan print squares and 29 — 2½" green print squares.

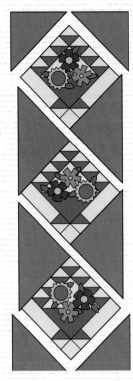

4. Sew together 22 green/tan print half-square triangle units in a row. Repeat to create a second row.

5. Sew together seven green/tan print half-square triangle units in a row, then sew a 1½" tan print square to each end of the row. Repeat to create a second row.

6. Measure the strips from step 4 through the center, then measure the quilt center from top to bottom through the center. Trim the top and bottom of the quilt center to match the measurement of the strips from step 4.

7. Measure the strips from step 5 through the center — *not* including the plain tan print squares — then measure the quilt center from side to side through the center. Trim the sides of

the quilt center to match the measurement of the half-square triangle unit strips from step 5 plus ½".

8. Referring to the quilt assembly diagram on Page 61 sew the side border strips to the quilt center. Press seams toward the quilt center.

9. Referring to the quilt assembly diagram, sew the top and bottom border strips to the quilt top. Press seams toward the quilt center.

10. Measure the quilt top from top to bottom through the center, then cut two brown/black print border strips to match that measurement. (They should measure 2¼" x 24½".) Referring to the quilt assembly diagram, sew those two strips to the sides of the quilt top. Press seams toward the border.

11. Measure the quilt top from side to side through the center, including the border strips just added, then cut two brown/black print border strips to match that measurement. (They should measure 2¼" x 13".) Referring to the quilt assembly diagram, sew those two strips to the top and bottom of the quilt top. Press seams toward the border.

12. Sandwich the quilt top, batting and backing; baste. Quilt as desired, then bind.

PETALS *in the* WIND

Designed and pieced by Vicki Olsen
Quilted by Dan Kolbe

Finished quilt size:
78½" x 90½"

I had so much fun laying out this quilt, thinking that the gold fabrics would make a Churn Dash block pop. But once everything came together, I saw flower petals everywhere, hence this quilt's title!

Fabric Requirements

- ◈ 4½ yards total of assorted light prints for rows
- ◈ 1⅔ yards total of assorted medium to dark prints for rows
- ◈ ½ yard each of four gold prints for rows
- ◈ ½ yard red print 1 for rows
- ◈ 1¼ yards red print 2 for border
- ◈ 5½ yards fabric of choice for backing
- ◈ ⅞ yard red print 2 for binding

Cutting Instructions

From assorted light prints, cut:
- ◈ 28 — 2½" strips the width of fabric, then sub-cut those into 434 — 2½" squares for rows
- ◈ 3 — 4½" strips the width of fabric, then sub-cut those into 44 — 2½" x 4½" rectangles for rows
- ◈ 15 — 4½" strips the width of fabric, then cut those into 120 — 4½" squares for rows

From medium to dark prints, cut:
- ◈ 23 — 2½" strips the width of fabric, then sub-cut those into 362 — 2½" squares for rows

From gold prints, cut:
- ◈ 18 — 2½" strips the width of fabric, then sub-cut those into 284 — 2½" squares for rows

From red print 1, cut:
- ◈ 5 — 2½" strips the width of fabric, then sub-cut those into 71 — 2½" squares for rows

From red print 2, cut:
- ◈ 9 — 4½" strips the width of fabric for border
- ◈ 9 — 3" strips the width of fabric for binding

Sewing Instructions

This quilt is assembled in rows instead of blocks.

ROW UNITS

1. Sew together a 2½" light print square and a 2½" medium to dark print square to create a Two-Patch unit. Repeat to create a total of 390 of these units.

2. Sew together 1 — 2½" light print square and 1 — 2½" red print 1 square. Repeat to create a total of 65 of these units.

3. Sew together two units from step 1 and one unit from step 2. Repeat to create a total of 65 of these units.

4. With right sides together, sew 1 — 2½" gold print square on the right side of 1 — 2½" x 4½" light print rectangle. Trim a ¼" seam allowance

off the gold square only, then press it back to create the unit shown in the far right diagram below. Repeat to create a total of 22 of these units.

5. With right sides together, sew 1— 2½" gold print square on the left side of 1 — 2½" x 4½" light print rectangle. Trim a ¼" seam allowance off the gold square only, then press it back to create the unit shown in the far right diagram below. Repeat to create a total of 22 of these units.

6. Sew together a 2½" dark print square, a unit from step 4, a 2½" light print square, and a unit from step 5. Repeat to make a total of 10 of these units.

7. With right sides together, sew 2 — 2½" gold print squares to opposite corners of a 4½" light print square. Repeat to make a total of 120 of these units.

8. Sew together a unit from step 7, a Two-Patch unit, a unit from step 7, and a Two-Patch unit, noting the orientation of each unit. Repeat to make a total of 60 of these units.

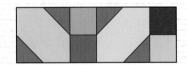

ROW ASSEMBLY

1. Referring to the following diagram, sew together 17 Two-Patch units and a 2½" light print square to create a Row A. Repeat to make a total of two Row As.

2. Referring to the following diagram, sew together two Two-Patch units, five units from step 6 of the Row Units section, and a 2½" dark print square to create a Row B. Repeat to make a total of two Row Bs.

3. Referring to the following diagram, sew together five units from step 3 of the Row Units section, two Two-Patch units, and a 2½" light print square to create a Row C. Repeat to make a total of seven Row Cs.

4. Referring to the following diagram, sew together three Two-Patch units, five units from step 8 of the Row Units section, one unit from step 4 of the Row Units section, and one unit from step 5 of the Row Units section. Repeat to create a total of 12 Row Ds.

5. Referring to the following diagram, sew together two Two-Patch units, five units from step 3 of the Row Units section, and a 2½" red print 1 square to create a Row E. Repeat to create a total of six Row Es.

QUILT ASSEMBLY

1. Referring to the quilt assembly diagram on Page 70, join the rows from steps 1–5 in the Row Assembly section, noting the different orientations of Rows B and D. (In some cases, they are positioned as shown in the diagrams in steps 2 and 4 of the Row Assembly section and in other cases, they are positioned upside down.) The quilt center should measure 70½" x 82½".

2. Sew the 2 — 4½" x 82½" black print border strips to the sides of the quilt center. Then sew the 2 — 4½" x 78½" black print border strips to the top and bottom of the quilt top.

3. Sandwich the quilt top, batting and backing; baste. Quilt as desired, then bind.

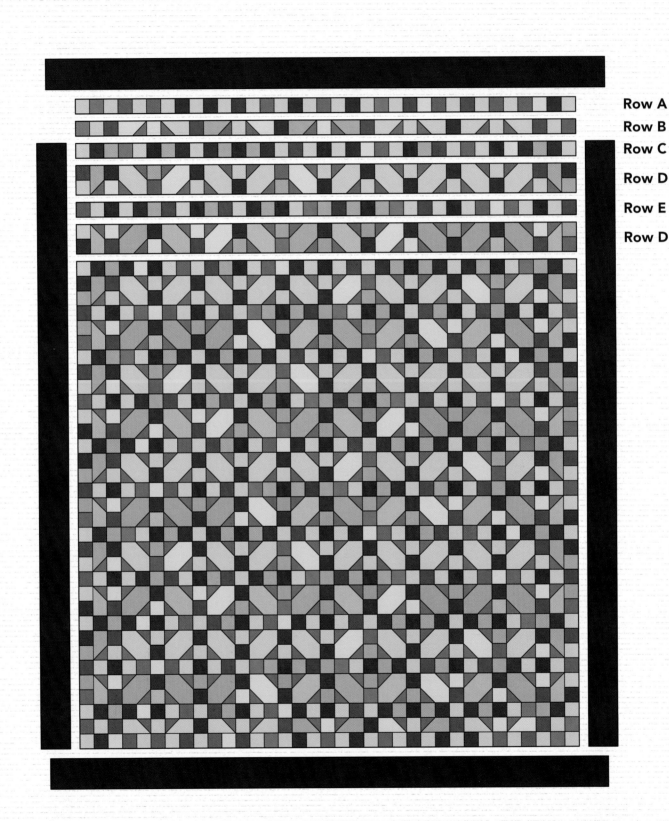

Row A

Row B

Row C

Row D

Row E

Row D

Quilt Assembly Diagram

STEPPING BACK IN TIME

Designed and pieced by Jill Shaulis

Large version finished size: 13" x 13" (not including frame)

Small version finished size: 11" x 11" (not including frame)

My fascination with small quilt pieces took on new meaning when I began foundation piecing a Pineapple block featured in our first book, Kindred Spirits. I couldn't stop there, so I created these two designs that showcase the classic Courthouse Steps block, using prints that evoke the past. I enjoy displaying small projects like these in rustic frames custom-made by my brother-in-law.

Fabric Requirements

I made one version (pictured on Page 72) with four 4" blocks and a smaller version (pictured on Page 76) with nine 2" blocks. Yardage requirements for the smaller version are listed in parentheses below.

◆ 7" square each of six different light prints for block squares and strips (4" square each of 12 different light prints)
◆ 7" square each of six different dark fabrics for block squares and strips (4" square each of 12 different dark prints)
◆ 2" black print for block centers (3" square)
◆ ¼ yard black print for border (⅛ yard)

Cutting Instructions

The cutting instructions for the smaller version are in parentheses below.

From each dark and light print, cut:
◆ 9 — ¾" x 7" strips for block squares and strips (9 — ⅜" x 4 strips)

From dark print, cut:
◆ 4 — 1" squares for block centers (9 — ⅝" squares)

From black print, cut:
◆ 2 — 3" x 8½" strips for border (2 — 3" x 6½" strips)
◆ 2 — 3" x 13½" strips for border (2 — 3" x 11½" strips)

Sewing Instructions

BLOCKS

1. Print four paper patterns on Pages 77 and 78 for the larger version or nine paper patterns on Page 79 for the smaller version. (Instead of paper, I prefer a product called Fundation made especially for foundation-piecing.)

2. Cut each pattern apart just outside the dashed lines.

3. Set your sewing machine's stitch length to 1.5.

4. For the small version, assign each dark print one of these letters: A, B, C, H, I, J, O, P, Q, V, W or X and each light print one of these letters: D, E, F, G, K, L, M, N, R, S, T or U as shown in the paper patterns. For the larger version, assign each dark print one of these letters: C, D, E, H, I or J and each light print one of these letters: A, F, B, G, F, K or L as shown in the paper patterns.

5. Place the paper, printed side down. Center a black print square over the #1 center square on the paper pattern. (Depending on your chosen foundation-piecing paper product, you might have to hold it up to a light source to ensure it is centered.) With right sides together, lay a light print strip that coordinates with the letter on the same side of the #2 square on the center square, matching the raw edges. (The light print strip needs to extend at least ¼" beyond the area to be covered.) If you find it helpful, you can pin the pieces in place as you sew them down to the paper pattern. Turn the paper pattern over and sew the line between the #1 square and #2 square, extending the sewing line a

stitch or two beyond the intersection. Trim the strip close to the ends of the stitched line.

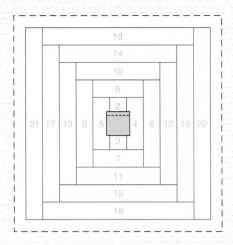

6. Turn the paper pattern over and finger press the #2 square out. Turn the paper pattern, print side down, again and continue adding fabric pieces, following the number order on the pattern. (All numbers that point north and south use light prints, while all numbers that point east and west use dark prints.) Be sure that the last round of strips extends beyond the dashed line in the paper pattern.

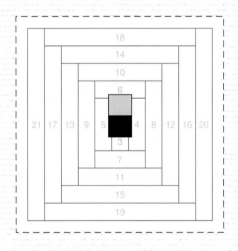
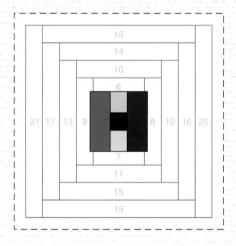
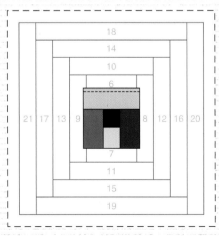
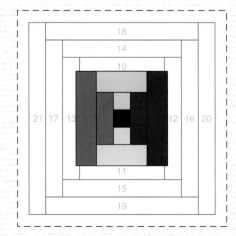

7. To hold the last strip in place when stitching blocks together later, stitch around the entire block so it falls between the last solid line and the dashed line. Trim the block on the dashed line of the paper pattern.

8. Repeat steps 2–7 to make a total of four blocks for the larger version and a total of nine blocks for the smaller version.

QUILT ASSEMBLY
Measurements for the smaller version are listed in parentheses below.

1. Sew the blocks together, using the outer solid line as your seam allowance guide.

2. To reduce bulk, press the seams open.

3. Referring to the quilt assembly diagrams (right), sew the 2 — 3" x 8½" black print border strips (2 — 3" x 6½" border strips) to the sides of the quilt center.

4. Referring to the quilt assembly diagrams, sew the 2 — 3" x 13½" black print border strips (2 — 3" x 11½" border strips) to the top and bottom of the quilt top.

5. Instead of quilting these projects, I framed them by wrapping the border 1½" on each side around the inner frame board and taping it to the back. To disguise the back and create a nice finished look, I placed another board on top of it.

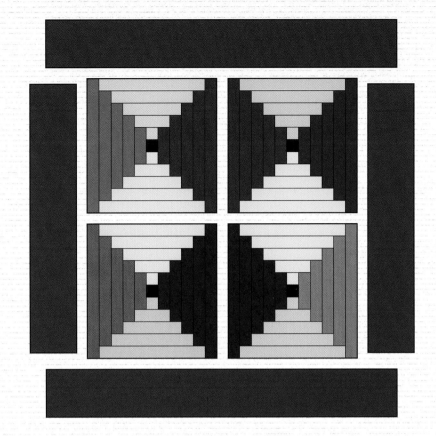

Assembly Diagram
Large Version

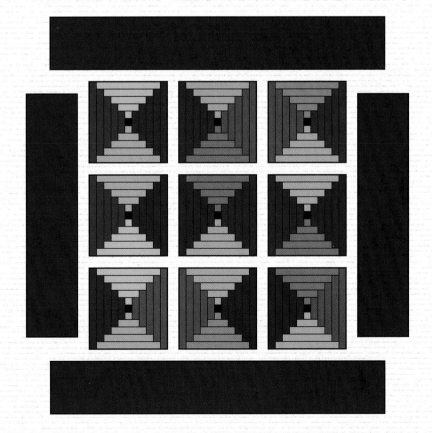

Assembly Diagram
Small Version

TIMEWORN CHARM
Spotlight your finished projects in our weathered barn-wood frames like those pictured on this page and Page 72. To order, contact Yellow Creek Quilt Designs at yellowcreekquiltdesigns@gmail.com or 815-443-2211.

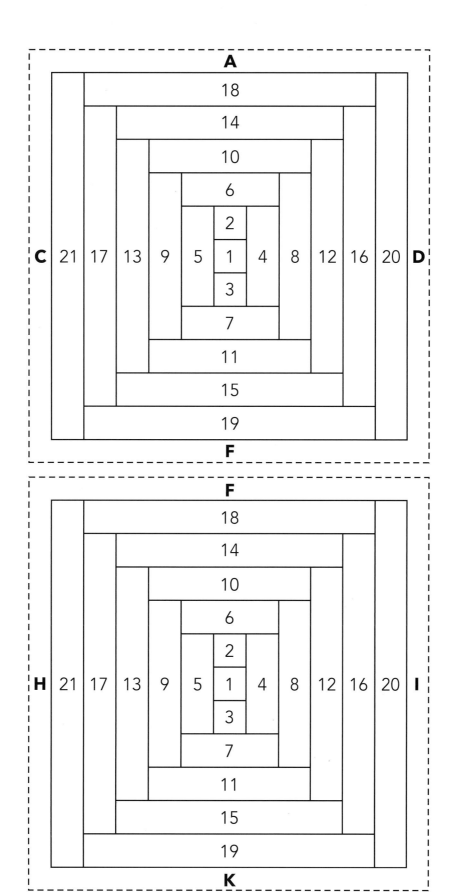

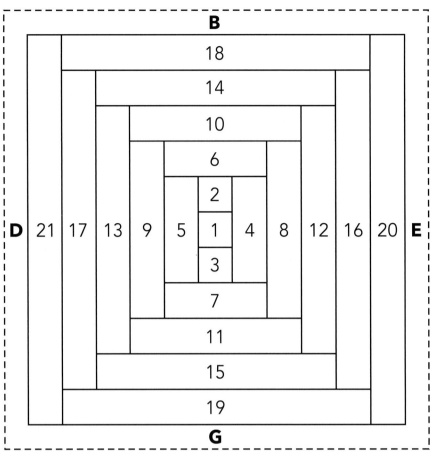

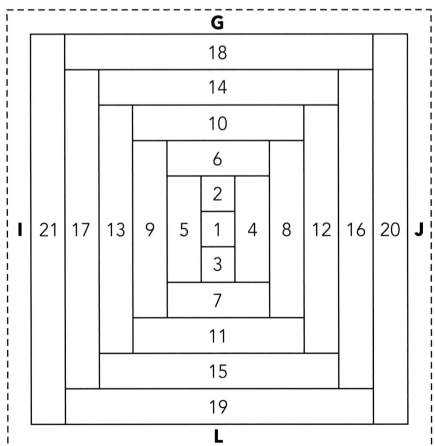

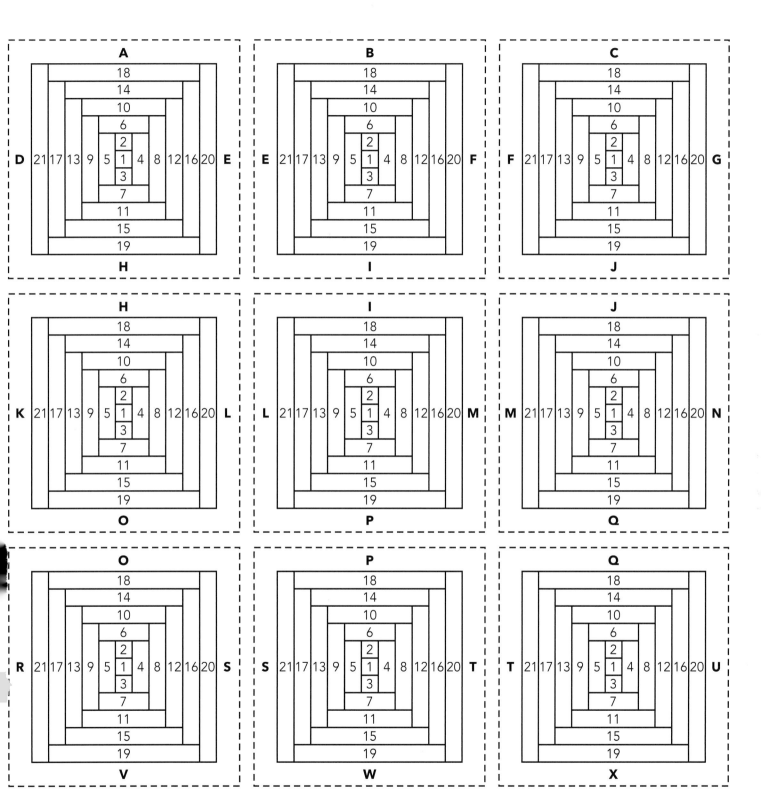